# BALLOON ANIMALS

### AARON HSU-FLANDERS

CB
CONTEMPORARY BOOKS

**The Library of Congress has cataloged an earlier printing as follows:**

Hsu-Flanders, Aaron.
     Balloon animals / Aaron Hsu-Flanders.
        p.    cm.
     ISBN 0-8092-4593-0
     1.  Balloon sculpture.    I. Title.
   TT926.H78     1988
   745.594—dc19          87-36578
                              CIP

32 33 34 35 36 37 38 39 40 41   BAH/BAH   2 1 0 9 8 7 6 5 4 3

ISBN 0-07-143474-7 (package)
ISBN 0-07-143742-8 (book)

Photos by David Caras, Boston, MA

McGraw-Hill books are available at special quantity discounts to use as premiums and sales promotions, or for use in corporate training programs. For more information, please write to the Director of Special Sales, Professional Publishing, McGraw-Hill, Two Penn Plaza, New York, NY 10121-2298. Or contact your local bookstore.

This book is printed on acid-free paper.

# CAUTION:

Although you will sometimes see professional balloon twisters use their mouths to form balloon bubbles, *do not* put inflated, tied balloons in *your* mouth. Should a balloon pop while you are inhaling, bits of rubber could get caught in your throat. I *never* use my mouth to do anything other than blow up a balloon. In addition, I do not recommend allowing very young children—i.e., those likely to put the balloons into their mouths—to handle balloons. And children under the age of seven who wish to make balloons should do so under the supervision of a responsible adult.

**Introduction**      ix

**Before You Start**
A Few Remarks About the Balloons      2
Inflating the Balloon      4
Tying the Balloon      6
When the Balloon Is Inflated      9

**Beginner Balloon Animals**
Dog      12
Giraffe      22
Dachshund      27
Rabbit      31
Horse      36
Hat      41

**Intermediate Balloon Animals**
Mouse      46
Poodle      50
  Poodle Lying Down      52
  Poodle Sitting Up      54
Reindeer/Moose      56

Elephant     62
Snoopy     69
Swan     75

**Advanced Balloon Animals**
Two Lovebirds Kissing in a Heart     82
Octopus     91
Ram     95
Teddy Bear with a Tulip     103

**Building Your Repertoire**

**Mail-Order Sources**

# ACKNOWLEDGMENTS

I would like to thank and dedicate this book to Muriel and Staunton, my parents; Stella and Dede, my grandmothers; Rachel and Robin, my sister and sister-in-law; and Joshua, my brother, who helped shape me in such a way that I was even able to see a future in balloons; Cathy Mahar, my agent, who immediately thought it was a good idea; Stacy Prince and Deborah Brody, my editors, for their ever-present enthusiasm; Caytee and Windigo, my real-life cats, for being real-life cats; and, most of all, Lillian, my companion in life, who was with me in every way, throughout this project.

Special gratitude goes to Dr. Ivan Ciric, Alan Lewitz, Leonard Fein, Bernie Berkin, Genevieve Lewitz, Thomas Pearson, David Thomas, David Caras, Jeff Hunter, Bisse Bowman and her K–2 class of 1983–84, and to every child and adult who, for a brief moment, has smiled at one of my balloons.

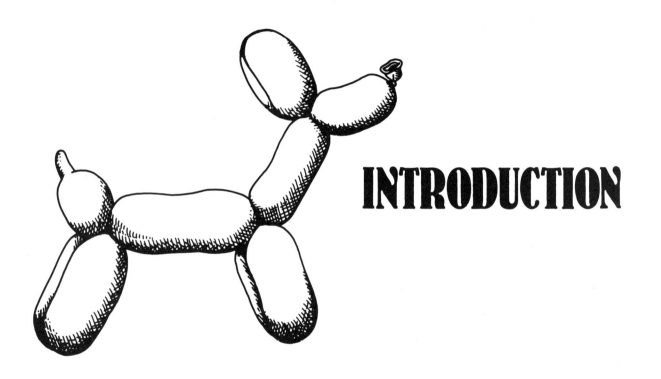

# INTRODUCTION

Children and adults have marveled over balloon animals for years, watching in awe as entertainers, with a few quick twists of their hands, transformed ordinary balloons into cute animals. But while balloon-animal twisting looks impressive and can make anyone a hero in a little kid's eyes, it isn't difficult. You merely need the right balloons, a pump (unless you've got really strong lungs), and step-by-step instructions, all of which are provided here. Even if you're all thumbs, you'll find you can make the basic animals and several of the fancier ones in just a few tries. With practice, you'll be able to create your own!

While you might be tempted to turn right to your favorite animal and get going, I'd suggest that you start at the beginning, with the dog. It is the easiest animal to make and will teach you the basic skills needed to construct the rest of the animals I've included. After the dog, try the giraffe; the animals are presented in order of difficulty, and it's best not to skip ahead too far. Be sure to read through the instructions on each animal before you begin, so you can avoid surprises—and trying to turn a page with your nose while your hands are full of half-twisted balloon!

This book comes with a "starter kit" of pencil balloons, but don't be alarmed it you're not an expert by the time the balloons run out. You'll get better with practice and will want to have a supply of balloons around. You might check your local toy store or a novelty, joke, or magic shop. Be sure to ask for the #260 variety. You can also order #260 balloons by mail; I've included a few mail-order suppliers at the back of the book.

Whether you intend to

use your new skill to
entertain your kids, bring
in a few extra bucks, or just
relieve stress (you wouldn't
believe how much better
you feel after making
yourself an animal friend or
two), I wish you years of
successful balloon
twisting—and lots of fun!

**BEFORE YOU START**

Be *sure* to make the balloons in the order they are presented in the book. If you skip ahead, you may have difficulty with twists and some of the more subtle positioning, which are explained in depth earlier in the book.

*Don't forget* to read all the directions for an animal thoroughly before making the first twist. Also be sure to read the section on inflating and tying a balloon.

Always start twisting your balloon animal at the end where you've tied it. In addition, try to hold the balloons as shown in the pictures, whether you are right- or left-handed. Switching around won't make it any easier, and the pictures will be more difficult to follow.

Any time a small bubble is called for, make a few extra twists to secure it. In general, the smaller the bubble, the more twists you need.

If you've gotten a twist wrong, play with the balloon to see if you can fix it. Start over. Allow your dog to have a snub nose. Don't worry if your giraffe's body turned out a little short. Use your imagination and ingenuity. Your animals don't have to look just like mine to be good.

# A FEW REMARKS ABOUT THE BALLOONS

Always make sure that your balloons are reasonably fresh. If you keep them in a dry place, away from heat, they should last a few months.

Keep your fingernails short and smooth. If you have sharp corners on your nails, you might need to file them down a bit so that they are more rounded. If you have long fingernails, you will just need to learn to keep your fingernails away from the balloons as you are twisting them.

Try to avoid twisting balloon animals in the sun. The direct sunlight and heat make the balloons susceptible to popping.

Remember that the balloons vary in size. If your balloon animal starts to look different from the one in the picture, it might be that your balloon is an inch or two shorter or longer than the one I used for the picture. If you notice that you're running out of uninflated balloon at the tip, make the last bubbles a little smaller than indicated. If you've got too much uninflated balloon at the tip, make the last bubbles a little larger. Experiment a bit. You may have to make a given animal a few times before you've got it down pat. If you have any doubts about bubble length or tail length, it's better to keep your balloon *proportions* the same as shown in the photographs than to try to measure the bubbles.

Balloons pop. While this doesn't happen as often as you might think (and *don't* be afraid to push and twist your balloons as directed, as they are made specifically for this purpose), it does happen, usually after a lot of handling. For that reason, it is wise to avoid twisting balloon animals anyplace where a sudden popping would be disturbing.

Although you may be tempted to draw on the balloons, I don't recommend it, as this greatly increases the chances of the balloon popping. If you cannot restrain yourself, use a felt-tip pen.

**Reminder:** DON'T put inflated, tied balloons in your mouth.

# INFLATING THE BALLOON

I recommend using the small hand pump included in this kit. For children or adults, these balloons are difficult to inflate with your own lungs, and the pump works quite well. Using the pump will also allow you to make as many balloon animals as you want, without getting tired from inflating them. Here are a few suggestions for inflating the balloons:

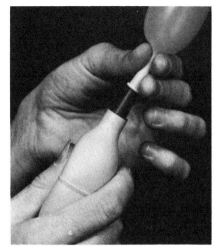

1. Stretch the balloon a few times before you inflate it. Slip the end of the balloon over the nozzle of the pump. Roll the neck of the balloon onto the nozzle about one inch. Hold it in place with the thumb and index finger of one hand. With your other hand, slowly begin inflating the balloon by squeezing and releasing the bulb of the pump.

**4**

**2.** Fill the balloon until there is an appropriate length of tail on the end. Each animal will require a specific amount of tail to be left at the end of the balloon when you inflate it. This tail will allow you to make many twists in the balloon. It allows the air in the balloon to expand as you make your twists.

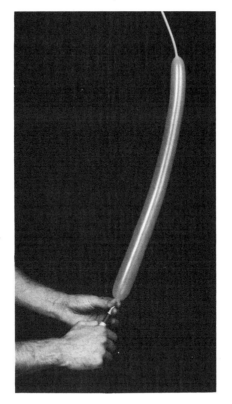

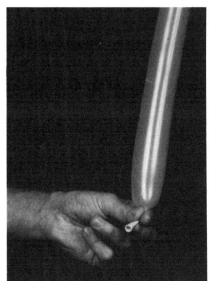

**3.** Slip the neck of the balloon off the nozzle of the pump, but continue pinching the neck of the balloon to keep the air inside.

# TYING THE BALLOON

There are many good ways to tie a balloon. Any way that works for you is fine. These are the steps that I follow:

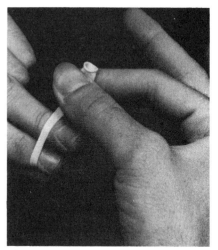

**1.** Let a tiny bit of air out of the balloon so that the neck of the balloon is a little longer and more flexible. Hold the neck of the balloon between your thumb and index finger.

**2.** Stretch the neck of the balloon over the backs of your index and middle fingers.

6

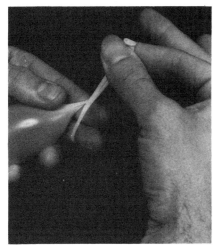 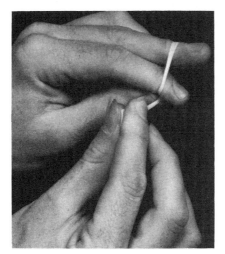 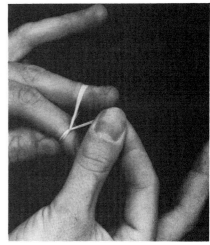

**3.** Continue stretching the neck of the balloon around the fronts of your index and middle fingers.

**4.** If you separate your index and middle fingers, you will create a small space.

**5.** Push the neck of the balloon through this space.

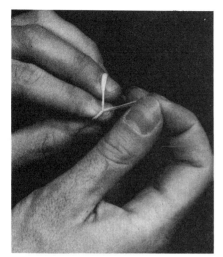

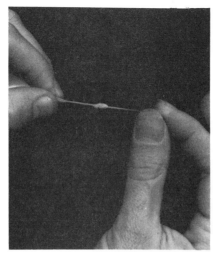

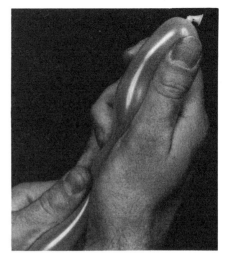

**6.** Holding the neck of the balloon, slide the rest of the balloon off your index and middle fingers.

**7.** Give a little tug, and you have your knot.

**8.** Before you begin twisting any of the animals in this book, squeeze each balloon gently at the knot end, to lessen the tension of the balloon behind the knot.

# WHEN THE BALLOON IS INFLATED

Don't run your hands up and down the sides of the balloon. Besides making a loud squeaking noise, this will weaken the sides of the balloon, and could cause it to pop.

Keep your inflated balloon away from any sharp objects. If you are wearing any sharp rings on your fingers, I suggest putting them in your pocket until you are finished twisting.

**BEGINNER BALLOON ANIMALS**

# DOG

To make most of the different animals, a balloon-animal maker needs to know one basic pattern of twisting. You will learn this twisting-and-locking pattern in making the dog and use it again and again in making all of the animals in this book. This pattern is repeated three times in making the dog. Pay careful attention to these twists before you try making any of the other animals. Being comfortable with this pattern of basic twists will help you in making some of the more difficult animals in this book.

Here's how to make the dog:

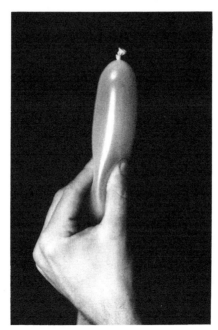

about three inches from the knot. You will begin twisting the balloon from the end that has the knot and twist toward the end that has the tail. This will allow the air in the balloon to move downward toward the tail as you make your twists.

**1.** Inflate the balloon and leave a 3-inch tail on the end.

**2.** Pinch the balloon with the thumb and index finger of one hand,

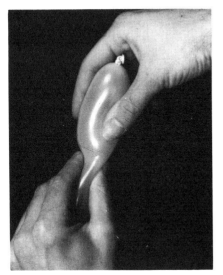

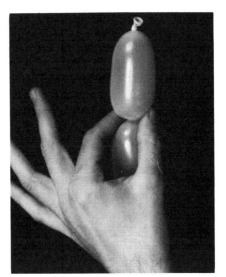

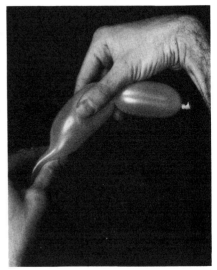

**3.** With your free hand, twist the 3-inch section of balloon around, two full turns, away from your body. This twist forms the nose of your dog.

**4.** Hold onto this twist gently with the thumb and index finger of one hand. This prevents it from untwisting.

**5.** While holding onto your first twist so that it doesn't untwist, pinch the balloon three inches below that 3-inch bubble. Twist both hands in opposite

**14**

directions until the balloon twists again. This second bubble forms one of the ears of your dog.

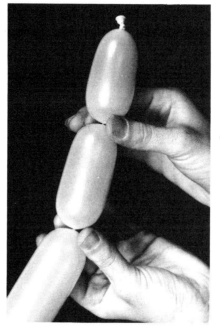

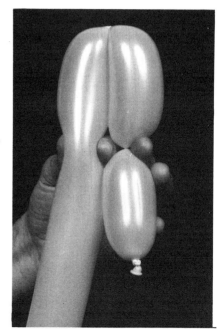

**6.** Keep holding onto both twists so that they don't untwist.

**7.** Now fold the two bubbles down alongside the length of the balloon.

Pinch the length of the balloon at the point where it meets your first twist. This will form the second ear of your dog.

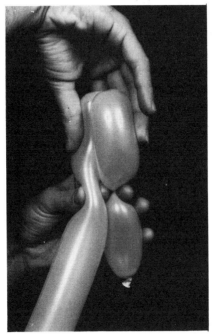

**8.** Twist both ears by rotating them together, about two full turns.

**9.** This third twist locks the first two twists of your animal, and

**16**

allows you to let go of the nose-and-ears section of your dog. Your hands are now free to finish the rest of your dog. This twist will be referred to throughout the book as the *locking twist*.

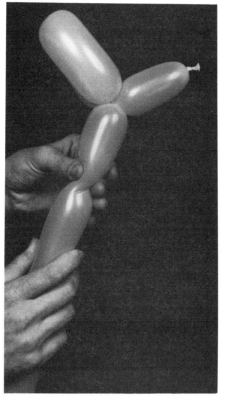

**17**

10. With the nose-and-ears section of your dog finished and locked into place with a *locking twist*, pinch the balloon with the thumb and index finger of one hand, about three inches below the nose-and-ears section. Holding one hand above and one hand below this point on the balloon, turn both hands in opposite directions until the balloon twists. This bubble will be the neck of your dog.

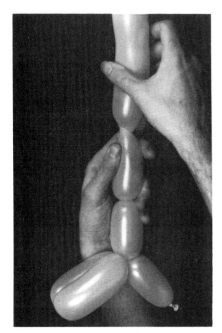

hand, and measure another three inches below your first twist, just as you did before. Turn both hands in opposite directions until the balloon twists again (at least two full turns). Hold onto both twists to make sure that they don't untwist. This second bubble will be one of your dog's front legs.

**11.** Gently hold this twist with the thumb and index finger of one

**12.** Fold these two bubbles down alongside the remaining length of balloon. Pinch the length of balloon at the point where it meets the first twist. These will be the two front legs of your dog.

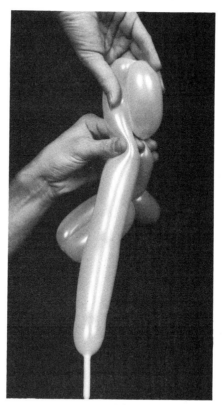

**13.** Twist both of the front legs around, using a *locking twist*, two full turns. This locks all three twists and frees your hands to finish the rest of your dog. You have just made the neck and front legs of your dog.

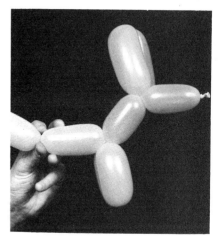

**14.** Beneath the neck-and-front-legs section of your animal, pinch off another 3-inch bubble. Twist the balloon again at this point, and hold this twist with one hand. This will be the body of your dog.

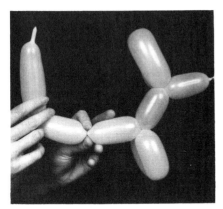

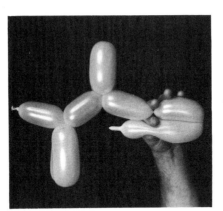

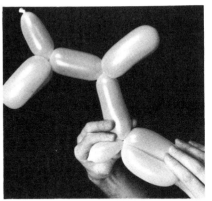

**15.** With your other hand, pinch off another 3-inch bubble below the one that you have just made. Make a twist in the balloon at this point. This second bubble will form one of your dog's back legs. Keep holding onto both twists.

**16.** Fold these two bubbles down alongside the remaining length of balloon. Pinch the last length of the balloon at the point where it meets your first twist. This bubble will form the other back leg of your dog.

**17.** Using a *locking twist*, twist both of the back legs around two full turns. This locks the body-and-back-legs section. Be sure to leave a little bubble at the very end for the dog's tail.

**20**

**18.** Play with the different parts of your balloon dog until it looks like the dog in the photo. Don't worry if your proportions are a little off; you'll get better with practice.

Congratulations! You have just made your first balloon creation.

# GIRAFFE

The giraffe is basically the same as the dog, but with a longer neck. You will make the same twists as you did for the dog, but you will make the neck longer, and all of the other body parts slightly smaller.

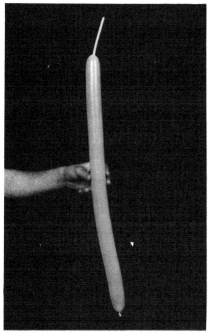

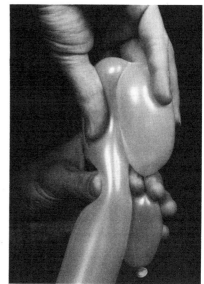

**1.** Begin by inflating the balloon and leaving a 4-inch tail on the end.

**2.** Starting at the end that has the knot, make two 3-inch bubbles, and fold them down alongside the length of the balloon.

**3.** Join them with a *locking twist*, the way you did with the dog's nose and ears.

**23**

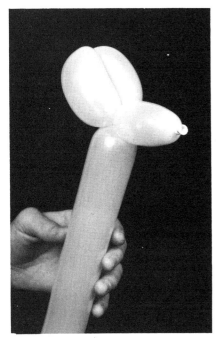

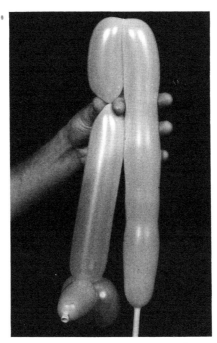

bubble for the neck. Follow this with a 3-inch bubble, and fold them both down alongside the length of the balloon.

**4.** This is what the giraffe's nose and ears look like.

**5.** Beneath the nose-and-ears section of your giraffe, make an 8-inch

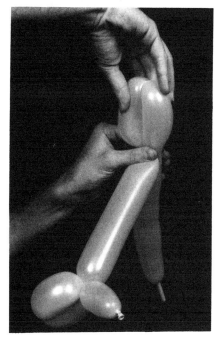

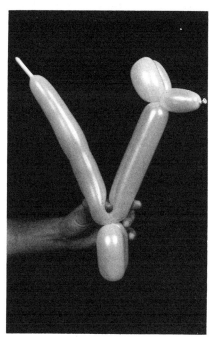

look like. The front and back legs of the giraffe are slightly smaller than those of the dog, to allow for the extra balloon that you will need for the 8-inch bubble for the neck.

**6.** Join them with a *locking twist.*

**7.** This is what the giraffe's nose, ears, neck, and front legs

**8.** Beneath the neck-and-front-legs section, make one 2-inch bubble and one 3-inch bubble. Fold them down alongside the remaining length of balloon.

**9.** Join them with a *locking twist*. Be sure to leave a little bubble for the tail.

**10.** This is a balloon giraffe.

# DACHSHUND

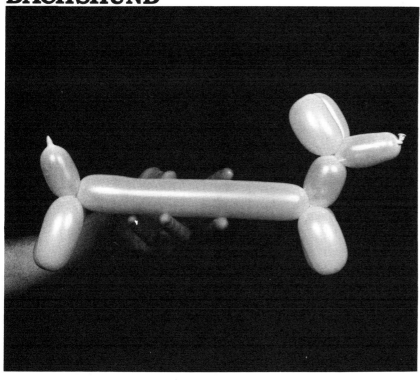

The dachshund is also similar to the dog, but it has a longer body section.

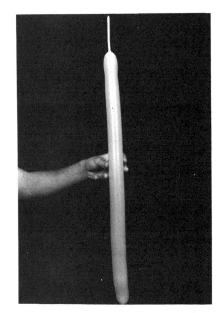

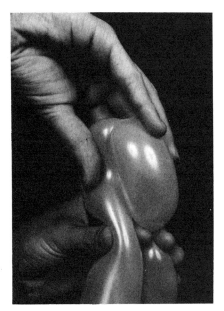

**1.** Inflate the balloon and leave a 4-inch tail on the end.

**2.** Begin by making two 3-inch bubbles, and folding them down alongside the length of the balloon.

**3.** Join these bubbles with a *locking twist*. These are the nose and ears of the dachshund.

**28**

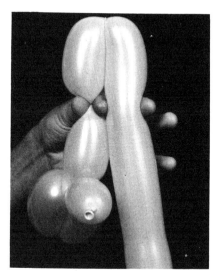

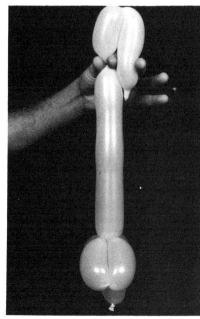

**4.** Make one 2-inch bubble and one 3-inch bubble, and fold them down alongside the length of the balloon.

**5.** Join these bubbles with a *locking twist*. This completes the nose, ears, neck, and front legs of the dachshund.

**6.** Make one 8-inch bubble for the body, followed by a 3-inch bubble for one of the back legs. Fold these two bubbles down alongside the remaining length of balloon.

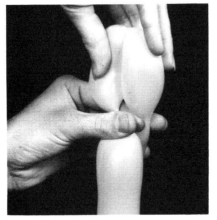

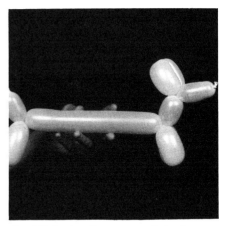

**7.** Join these bubbles with a *locking twist*. Be sure to leave a small bubble for the tail.

**8.** This is the completed balloon dachshund.

# RABBIT

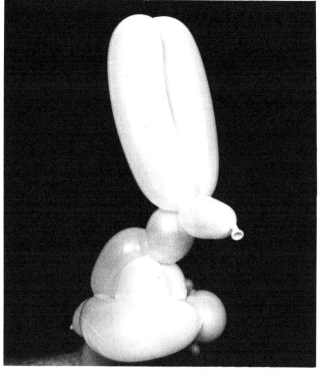

The rabbit is an interesting variation of the dog.

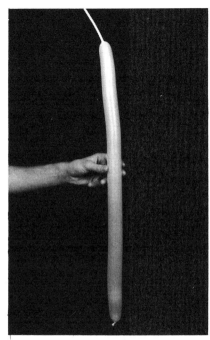

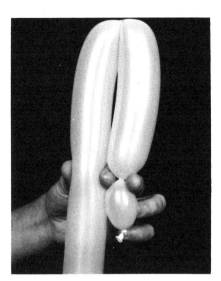

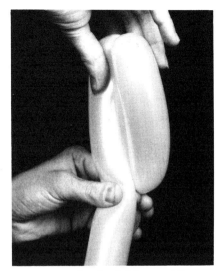

**1.** Begin by inflating the balloon and leaving a 4-inch tail.

**2.** Make a 2-inch bubble for the nose, followed by a 6-inch bubble for one of the ears. Fold both of these bubbles down alongside the length of balloon.

**3.** Join the bubbles with a *locking twist*, forming the nose and long ears of the rabbit.

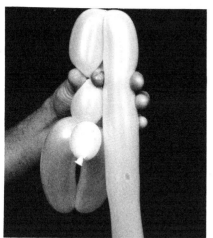

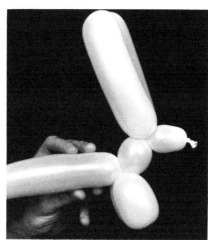

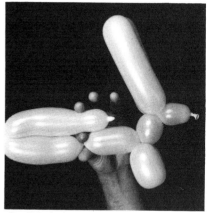

**4.** Make a 2-inch bubble for the neck of the rabbit, followed by a 3-inch bubble for one of the front legs. Fold these two bubbles down alongside the length of the balloon.

**5.** Join the bubbles with a *locking twist*. This forms the neck and front legs of the rabbit.

**6.** Make a 2-inch bubble for the body, followed by a 4-inch bubble for one of the back legs. Fold both of these bubbles down alongside the remaining length of balloon.

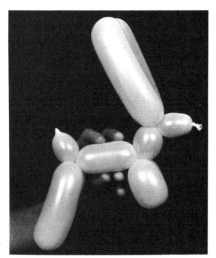

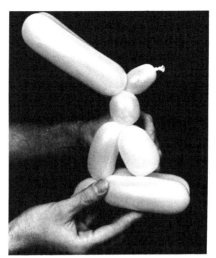

**7.** Join these bubbles with a *locking twist.* This forms the rabbit's body and back legs. Be sure to leave a little bubble for the tail.

**8.** To get the rabbit to sit up, push the rabbit's front legs down in between the back legs.

**9.** Spread the back legs apart and roll them around the front legs. Be sure not to force the front legs into the back legs. *Roll* the back legs over and around the front ones.

**10.** This is the completed
balloon rabbit.

# HORSE

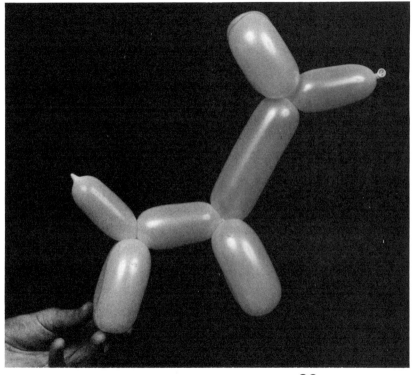

You'll get a lot of requests for this favorite animal.

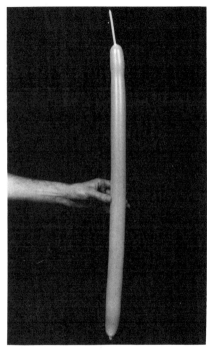

**1.** Inflate the balloon, leaving a 4-inch tail.

**2.** Begin by making a 3-inch bubble for the nose, followed by a 2-inch bubble for one of the ears.

**3.** Fold these two bubbles down alongside the length of the balloon.

**37**

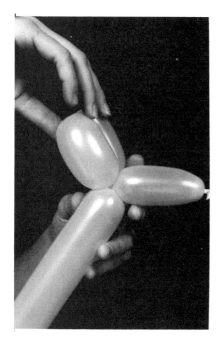 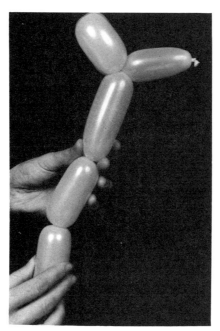 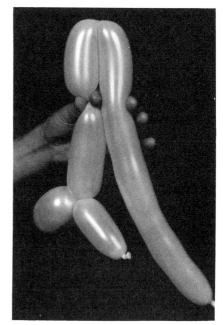

**4.** Join them with a *locking twist*, creating the nose and ears of your horse.

**5.** Make a 4-inch bubble for the neck, and a 3-inch bubble for one of the front legs.

**6.** Fold these two bubbles down alongside the length of the balloon.

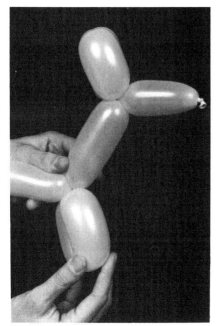

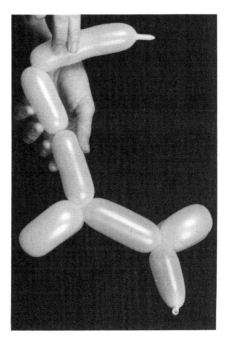

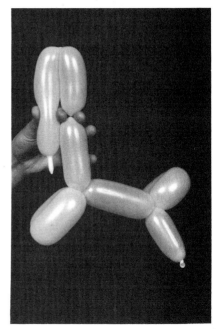

**7.** Join them with a *locking twist*, creating the neck and front legs of your horse.

**8.** Make a 3-inch bubble for the body, and a 3-inch bubble for one of the back legs.

**9.** Fold these two bubbles down alongside the remaining length of balloon.

**39**

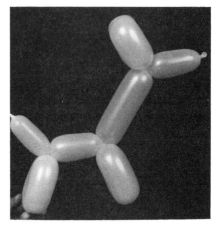

**11.** This is a balloon horse.

**10.** Join them with a *locking twist*, and be sure to leave a little bubble for the tail.

# HAT

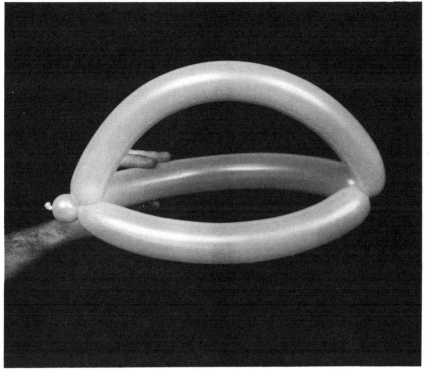

Use your imagination with this one! It is a great deal of fun to make up your own kinds of hats, and you can make some wonderful creations by using more than one balloon.

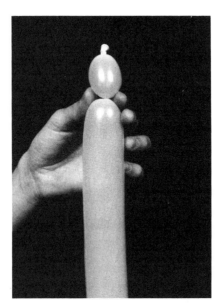

**1.** Inflate the balloon until you have a 1-inch tail. Tie a knot, and squeeze the balloon below the knot to release some tension in the balloon.

**2.** Make a 1-inch bubble below the knot. Hold onto it.

**3.** Wrap the balloon around the head of the person that you're making it for, and mark with your finger where the twist meets the balloon.

**42**

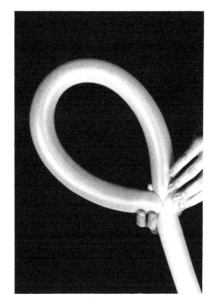 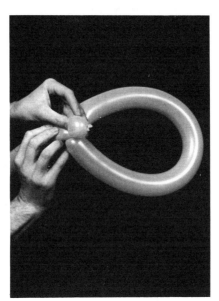 

**4.** Take the balloon off the person's head, and join the 1-inch bubble with the length of balloon at the point you've been marking.

**5.** Twist the 1-inch bubble all the way around this length of balloon until it locks.

**6.** Hold the tail end of the balloon, and pull it over to the opposite side of the hat, creating an arc.

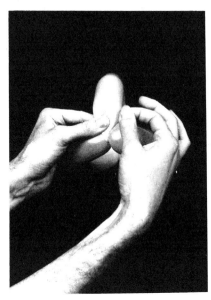

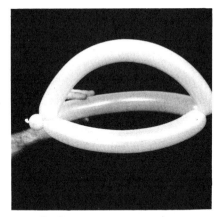

**8.** This is a balloon hat.

**7.** Wrap the tail around the body of the balloon two full times. This will lock it in place.

44

# INTERMEDIATE
# BALLOON ANIMALS

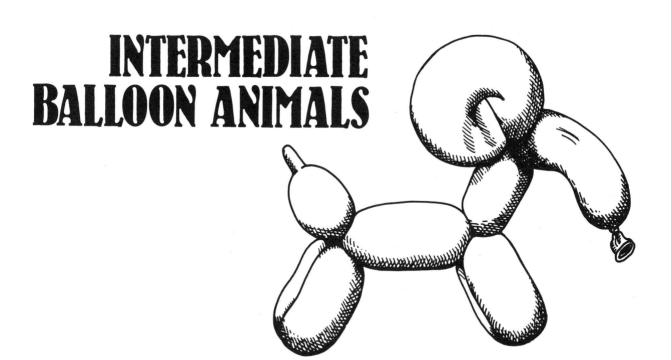

# MOUSE

The mouse is remarkably similar to the dog. In fact, the procedure is exactly the same, but all of the bubbles used in making the mouse are small (1-inch) bubbles, and you begin by inflating the balloon just 8 inches. You'll need to practice making 1-inch bubbles for this animal. It helps if you squeeze the tail end of the balloon a little, up toward the knot, while you're twisting your 1-inch bubbles, and remember to twist a few extra times for the smaller bubbles.

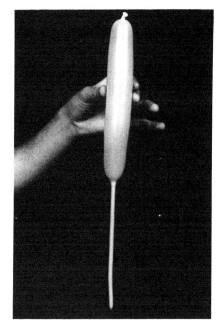

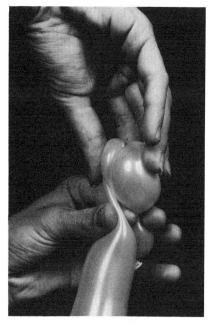

**1.** Begin by inflating the balloon until you have 8 inches of **air** (not tail) in the balloon.

**2.** Make two 1-inch bubbles and fold them down alongside the length of the balloon.

**3.** Join these bubbles with a *locking twist*. This forms the nose and ears of your mouse.

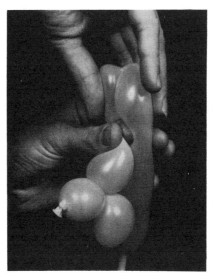

**4.** Make two more 1-inch bubbles below the nose-and-ears section, and fold them down alongside the remaining length of balloon.

**5.** Join these bubbles with a *locking twist*. This forms the neck and front legs of your mouse.

**6.** Make two more 1-inch bubbles with the very small remaining length of balloon. Fold these bubbles down alongside the very small length of balloon that's left.

**7.** Join these bubbles with a *locking twist.* Be sure to leave a small bubble for the beginning of the tail. This also helps to lock the last bubbles since they are so small.

**8.** This is a completed balloon mouse.

# POODLE

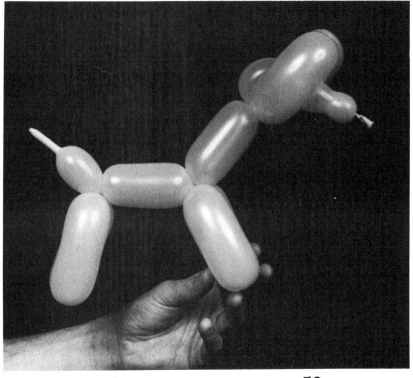

This is a multitalented animal! It's especially fun to make, because it can sit up and lie down.

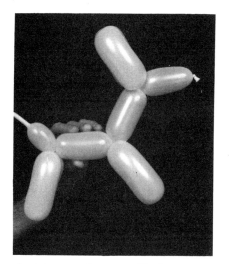

**1.** Begin the poodle by making a standard dog, as described earlier.

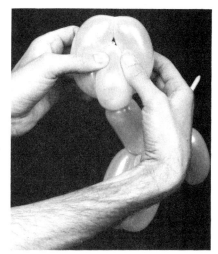

**2.** Now spread the ears apart and push the nose halfway through the ears.

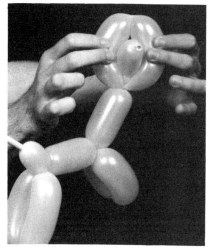

**3.** Gently roll the ears around the nose.

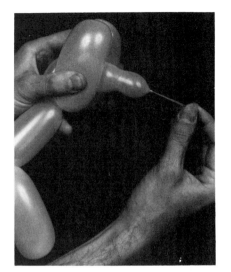

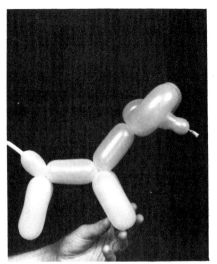

**4.** Squeeze the ears gently, and give a slight tug on the knot to release a little extra balloon at the knot. This also adds a little contour to the poodle's nose.

**5.** Turn the head around, and you have a finished balloon poodle.

Begin with the basic poodle that I have just described.

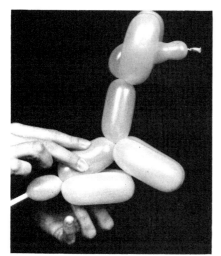

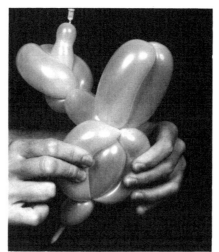

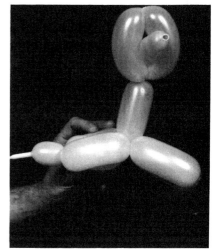

**1.** Push the body of the poodle down in between the back legs.

**2.** Gently spread the back legs of the poodle, and roll them around the body.

**3.** Position the head the way you like it best, and you have made your balloon poodle lie down.

# POODLE SITTING UP

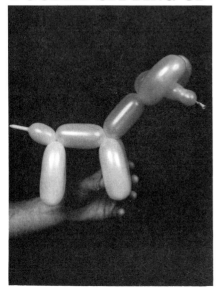

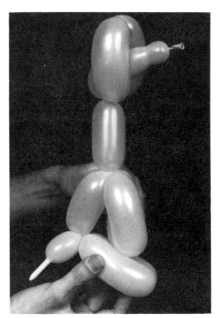

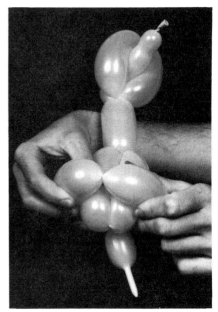

Begin by making the standard poodle described earlier.

**1.** This time, push the front legs down into the back legs.

**2.** Remember to roll the back legs around the front legs, just as you did with the rabbit. Don't force them.

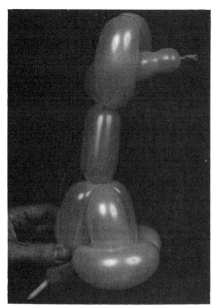

**3.** This is a balloon poodle
sitting up.

# REINDEER/MOOSE

Two animals for the price of one with a single extra twist!

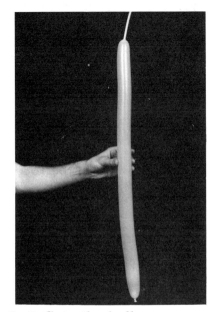

**1.** Inflate the balloon, leaving a 4-inch tail.

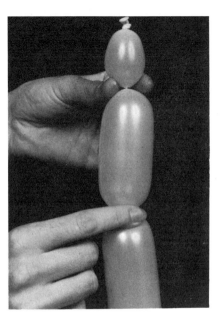

**2.** Begin the reindeer with a 2-inch bubble for the nose, followed by a 3-inch bubble.

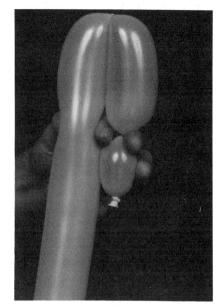

**3.** Fold these two bubbles down alongside the length of the balloon.

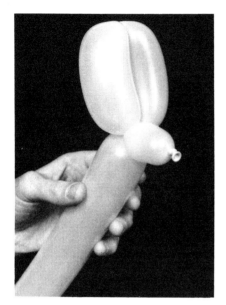

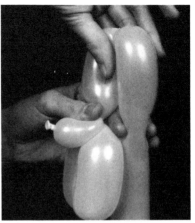

**4.** Join them with a *locking twist.*

**5.** Now make another 3-inch bubble, and fold the length of the balloon down alongside the 3-inch bubble that you just made.

**6.** Measure another 3-inch bubble along the length of balloon, to match the last one that you made. Join these two bubbles with a *locking twist* at their bases, to form a second set of antlers for the reindeer.

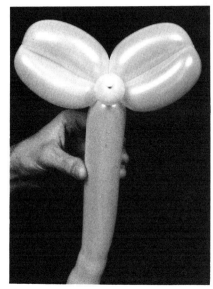

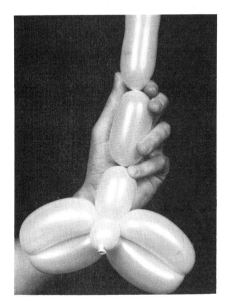

The second antler used up a little extra balloon in the reindeer's head. Make a 2-inch bubble for the neck, and a 4-inch bubble for one front leg.

**7.** This is what a balloon reindeer's head looks like.

**8.** The reindeer's body is the same as the dog's but the proportions are slightly smaller because you have less of the balloon to work with.

**9.** Fold these two bubbles down alongside the length of the balloon.

**10.** Join them with a *locking twist*. This forms the neck and front legs of the reindeer.

**11.** Make a 3-inch bubble for the body, and a 4-inch bubble for one back leg.

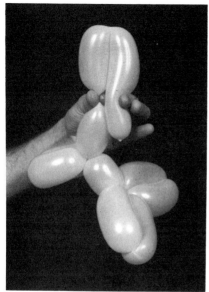

**12.** Fold these two bubbles down alongside the remaining length of balloon.

**13.** Join them with a *locking twist*. Be sure to leave a little bubble on the end for a tail. This is a balloon reindeer.

To make a balloon moose, simply twist the reindeer's antlers forward approximately ¼ turn, until they pop up to form a V.

# ELEPHANT

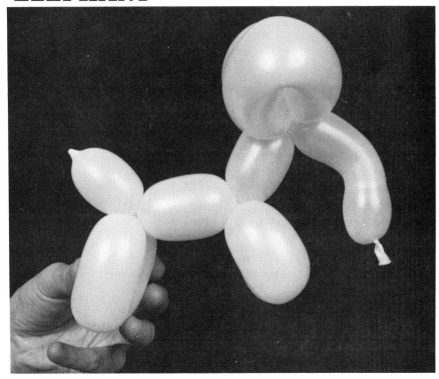

This is always a crowd pleaser!

**1.** Inflate the balloon, leaving a 5-inch tail.

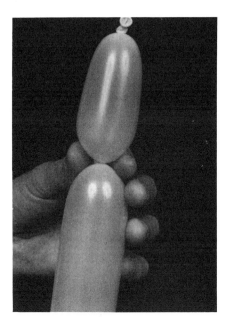

**2.** Begin by making a 3-inch bubble for the trunk.

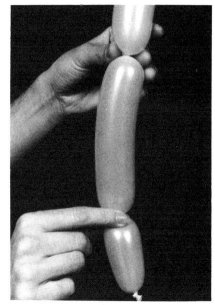

**3.** The next two bubbles, which will be the ears, are slightly different than the ears on the other animals that you

have made so far.
Elephant ears are made
by folding a 6-inch
bubble in half, and
joining it at its ends.
Make a 6-inch bubble.

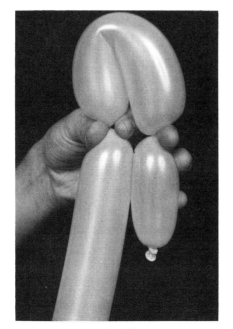

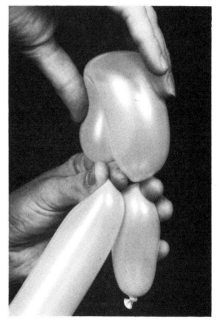

**4.** Fold it in half.

**5.** Twist it around on its ends until it locks.

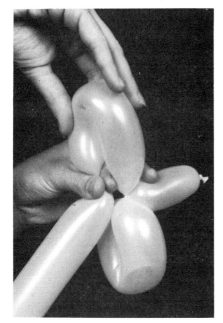

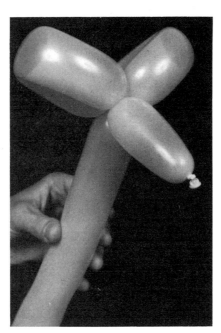

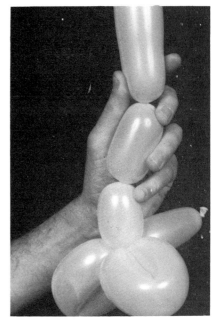

**6.** Repeat this process, with a second 6-inch bubble, for the second ear.

**7.** This is an elephant's head (so far).

**8.** Make a 2-inch bubble for the neck, and a 3-inch bubble for one front leg.

**65**

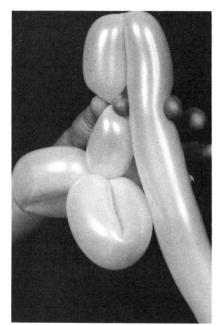

**9.** Fold these two bubbles down alongside the length of the balloon.

**10.** Join them with a *locking twist.*

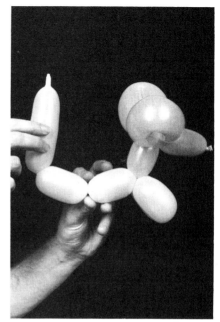

**11.** Make a 2-inch bubble for the body, and a 3-inch bubble for one back leg.

 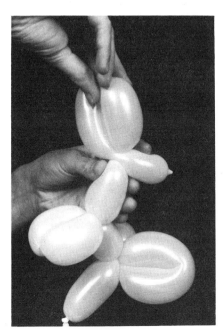 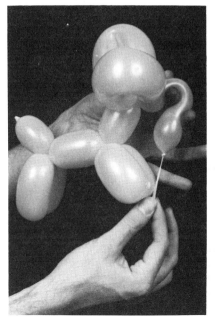

**12.** Fold these two bubbles down alongside the length of the balloon.

**13.** Join them with a *locking twist.* Leave a very small bubble for the tail.

**14.** Bend the trunk of the elephant in half and *gently* squeeze it with one hand. At the same time, give a *gentle* tug on the knot to release a little extra balloon at the knot.

**15.** Rub the bend in the trunk lightly. This will give a slight curve to the elephant's trunk.

**16.** This is a balloon elephant.

# SNOOPY

One of the world's most famous beagles!

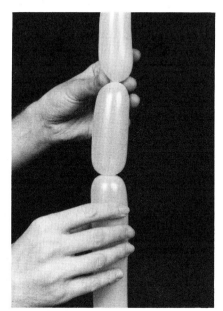

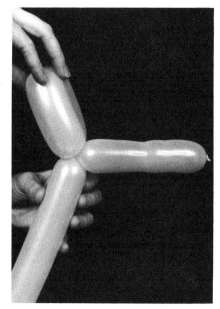

**1.** Inflate the balloon, leaving a 5-inch tail. Be sure to squeeze the balloon below the knot to lessen the tension.

**2.** Make a 7-inch bubble, followed by a 4-inch bubble.

**3.** Fold these two bubbles down alongside the length of the balloon, and join them with a *locking twist*.

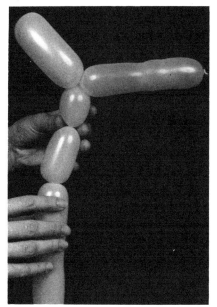

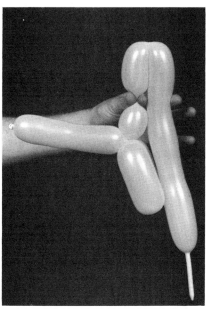

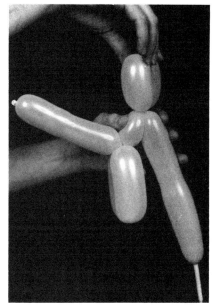

**4.** Make a 2-inch bubble for the neck, followed by a 3-inch bubble for one of the front legs.

**5.** Fold these two bubbles down alongside the length of the balloon.

**6.** Join them with a *locking twist*, creating the neck and front legs of your balloon Snoopy.

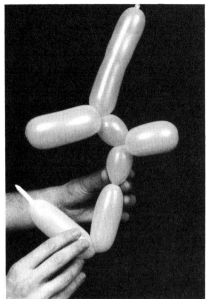

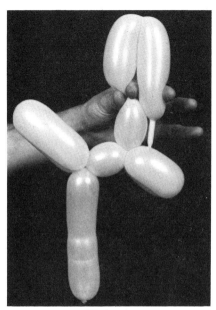

**7.** Make a 3-inch bubble for the body, followed by a 4-inch bubble for one of the back legs.

**8.** Fold these two bubbles down alongside the length of the balloon.

**9.** Join them with a *locking twist.* Be sure to leave a little bubble for the tail.

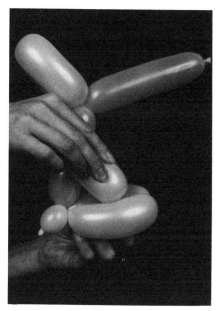 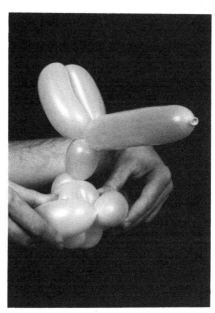 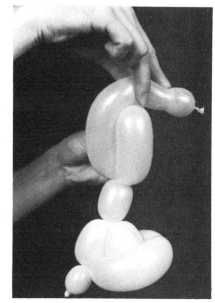

**10.** To make the animal sit up, push the front legs down into the back legs, just as you did with the rabbit.

**11.** Remember to roll the back legs around the front legs; don't force them.

**12.** Now take the 7-inch bubble that you've made for the nose, and bend it over the top of the two ears.

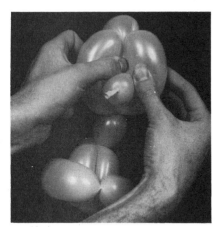

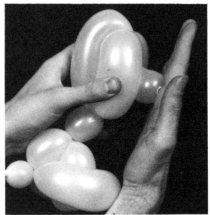

**13.** Gently pull the two ears apart from behind, and push the nose back in between the ears so that it is wedged in there, and stays by itself.

**14.** Gently squeeze the ears from the outside, and rub the tip of the nose upward at the same time, with the palm of your hand. Do this until you have created a little bend in the nose, and it points forward.

**15.** This is a balloon Snoopy.

# SWAN

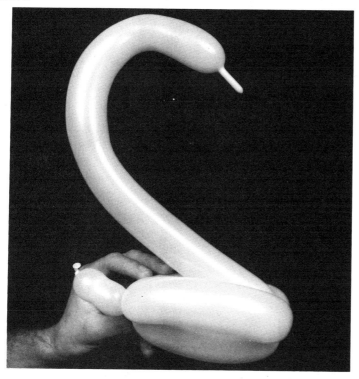

Try floating your swan in the bathtub!

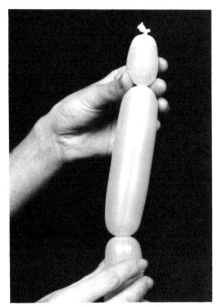

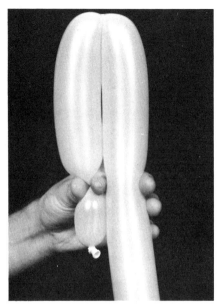

1. Inflate the balloon and leave a 3-inch tail on the end. Squeeze the balloon below the knot to lessen the tension.

2. Make a 1-inch bubble, followed by a 5-inch bubble.

3. Fold these two bubbles down alongside the length of the balloon.

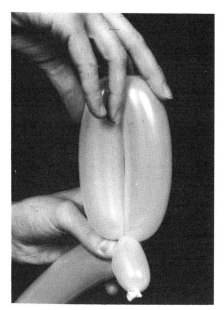

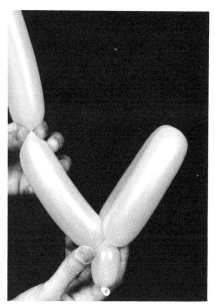

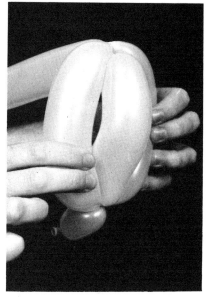

**4.** Join the bubbles with a *locking twist*.

**5.** Below this, make another 5-inch bubble.

**6.** Gently pull the first two 5-inch bubbles apart, and push the third 5-inch bubble between them.

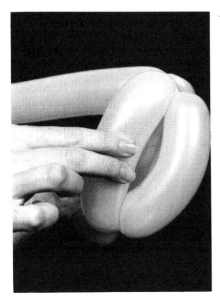

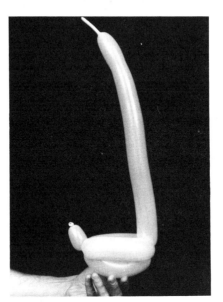

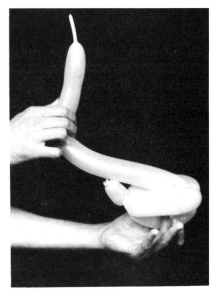

**7.** Roll the first two 5-inch bubbles around the third 5-inch bubble until the third bubble is all the way through the first two bubbles.

**8.** Hold the balloon so that two of the 5-inch bubbles are on top.

**9.** With one hand, gently separate these two bubbles, and pull the long length of balloon back between them.

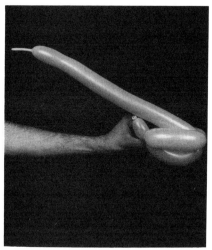

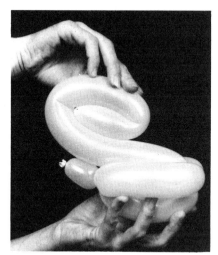

**10.** Press the length of the balloon snugly between the two bubbles until it stays in place and points straight backward.

**11.** Roll the long length of balloon up into a coil.

**12.** Roll the neck of the swan back and forth until the neck is shaped just right. This is a balloon swan.

# ADVANCED
# BALLOON ANIMALS

# TWO LOVEBIRDS
# KISSING IN A HEART

More fun than a traditional Valentine!

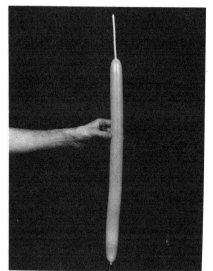

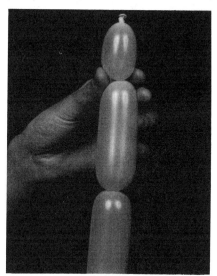

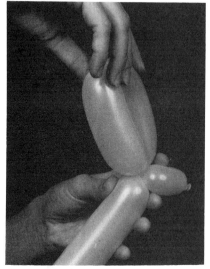

**1.** Inflate the balloon, leaving a 5-inch tail. Gently squeeze the knot end of the balloon before you make this animal, to lessen the tension in the balloon.

**2.** Make a 1½-inch bubble, followed by a 3-inch bubble.

**3.** Fold these two bubbles down alongside the length of the balloon, and join them with a *locking twist*.

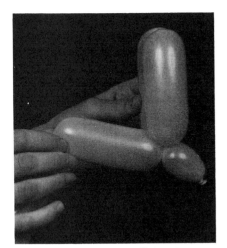

**4.** Make another 3-inch bubble.

**5.** Carefully spread the first two 3-inch bubbles apart, and roll them around the third 3-inch bubble. Push the third bubble gently through the two spread bubbles until it is all the way through.

**6.** This is what it looks like so far.

**84**

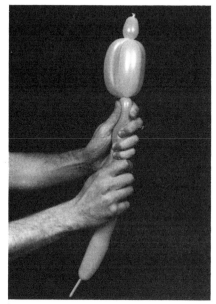 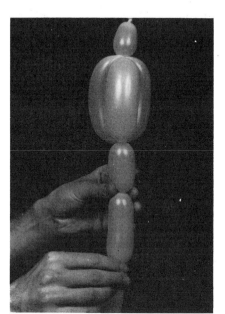 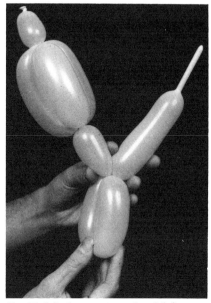

**7.** Now give the remaining length of balloon a gentle squeeze to lessen the tension.

**8.** Make a 2-inch bubble, followed by a 3-inch bubble.

**9.** Fold these two bubbles down alongside the remaining length of balloon and join them with a *locking twist*.

85

**10.** Fold the remaining length of balloon alongside the two 3-inch bubbles.

**11.** Pinch off whatever sticks above the 3-inch bubbles, and twist a small bubble out of it.

**12.** Tuck this bubble over and then through the 3-inch bubbles. This will join all three of the 3-inch bubbles.

**13.** Turn the balloon back over, and return to the 2-inch bubble in the middle.

**14.** Make a twist directly in the middle of the 2-inch bubble, forming two 1-inch bubbles.

**15.** Fold the balloon in half at the point between these two 1-inch bubbles.

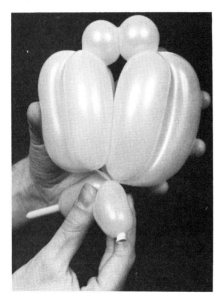

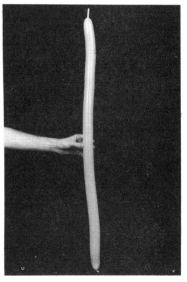

## PUTTING THE BIRDS IN A HEART

**16.** Return to the two loose bubbles at the other end of the balloon and twist them around each other until they lock.

**17.** Turn the balloon back over, and you have your two lovebirds kissing.

**1.** Inflate a balloon almost all the way to the end. Leave a 1-inch tail, and tie a knot.

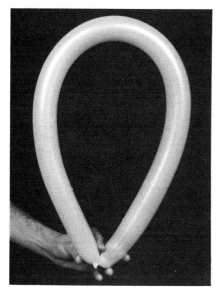

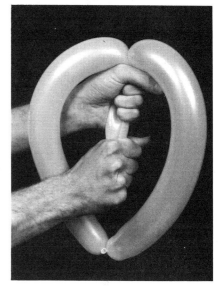

**2.** Tie another knot with the tail end and the knot end, to form a big balloon loop.

**3.** Double the balloon up, opposite the knot, and bring the doubled-up balloon all the way down to the knot.

**4.** Gently squeeze all of the air out of the doubled portion. Give a gentle tug on the balloon when the air has been squeezed out of it.

**5.** When you let go, the balloon will be somewhat heart-shaped. Work with this one to perfect it; it's not that hard.

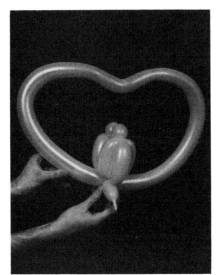

**6.** Place the lovebirds onto the knot of the heart, and twist the bottom bubbles of the lovebirds around the knot of the heart to secure it in place.

**7.** This is two balloon lovebirds kissing in a balloon heart.

# OCTOPUS

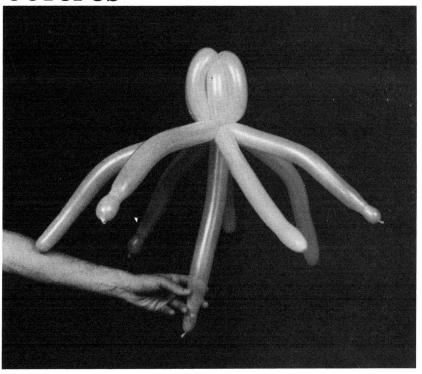

The octopus requires four balloons, and is a sensational balloon creature.

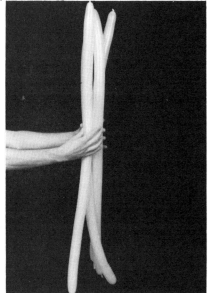

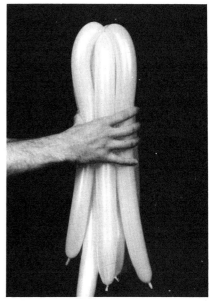

**1.** Begin by inflating four balloons, leaving a 1-inch tail on each of them. Line them all up next to each other.

**2.** With both hands, twist all four balloons together at their middle points. Twist them around a couple of times.

**3.** Now fold all eight arms downward, with the twist on top.

**4.** With both hands, measure down about ⅓ of the way from the first twist to the ends of the balloons, and twist all eight arms together at this point.

**5.** Twist them around a couple of times. This will take a little getting used to.

**6.** Give gentle tugs on all of the knots, to release a little tension, and gently squeeze the tail ends until the tails are filled up with air.

**7.** Shape the arms and legs of the octopus by folding each of them slightly and gently rubbing them at their folds. It helps to warm the folds with a little breath from your mouth.

**8.** This is a balloon octopus.

**94**

# RAM

This animal is one of my favorites. It's well worth the extra effort to learn it.

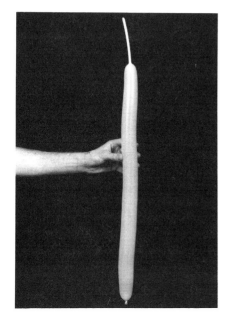

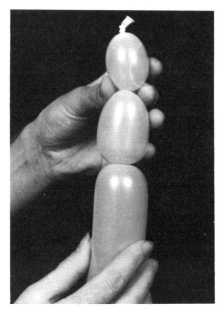

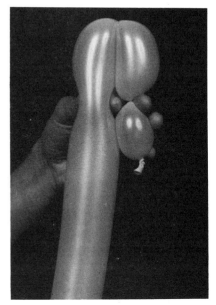

**1.** For this animal, you must leave a 5-inch tail on the end of the balloon when you inflate it.

**2.** Begin by making a 1-inch bubble for the nose, followed by a 2-inch bubble.

**3.** Fold these two bubbles down alongside the length of the balloon.

**96**

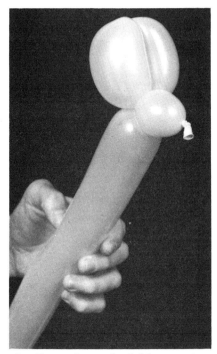

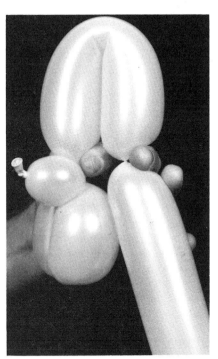

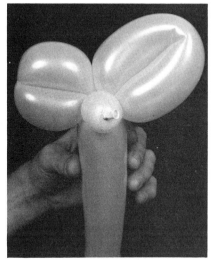

**6.** Join it on its ends with a *locking twist*.

**4.** Join these bubbles with a *locking twist*.

**5.** Make a 6-inch bubble and fold it in half.

**97**

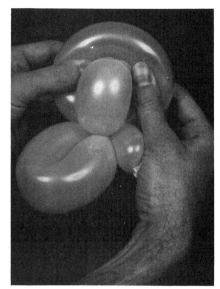

**7.** Do this again with a second 6-inch bubble. These will be the horns of your ram.

**8.** Take one of the folded bubbles and carefully roll it back over one of the 2-inch bubbles.

**9.** Gently push the 2-inch bubble into the folded bubble at the same time.

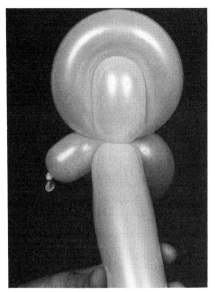

**10.** This is what one ram's horn looks like.

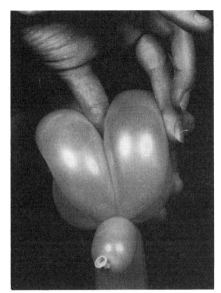

**11.** Repeat this process with the second folded 6-inch bubble.

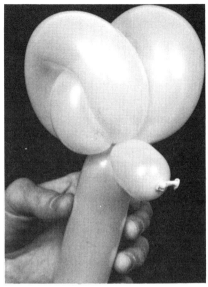

**12.** This is what a ram's head with both horns looks like.

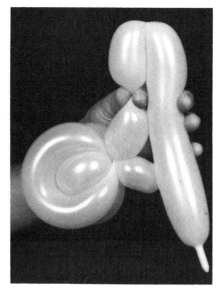

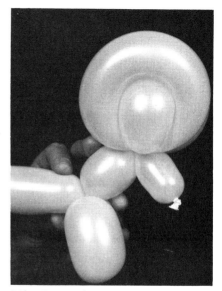

**13.** Make a 2-inch bubble for the neck, and a 2½ inch bubble for one of the front legs.

**14.** Fold these two bubbles down alongside the remaining length of the balloon.

**15.** Join them with a *locking twist.*

**16.** Make a 1½-inch bubble for the body of the ram, and a 2½-inch bubble for one of the back legs.

**17.** Fold these two bubbles down alongside the remaining length of balloon.

**18.** Join them with a *locking twist*. Remember to leave a little bubble on the end for a tail.

**19.** This is what a balloon ram looks like.

# TEDDY BEAR WITH A TULIP

This balloon animal is a real challenge. And who can resist a teddy bear?

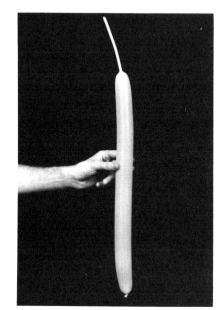

**1.** Inflate the balloon, leaving a 6-inch tail.

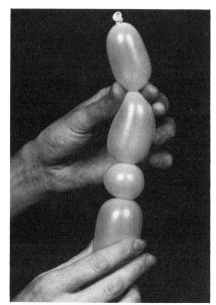

**2.** Make two 2-inch bubbles, followed by one 1-inch bubble.

**3.** Make another 2-inch bubble, followed by another 1-inch bubble, followed by another 2-inch bubble.

**104**

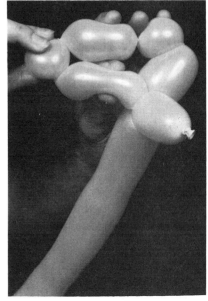

**4.** Fold the balloon over so that the first twist meets the last twist.

**5.** Join these two twists with a *locking twist.*

**6.** Pinch one of the 1-inch twists, and pull it out slightly from the adjoining 2-inch twists.

**105**

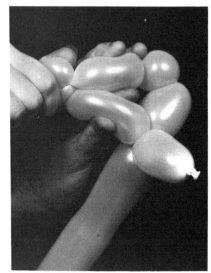

**7.** Twist the 1-inch bubble on its ends, and twist it around a couple of times.

**8.** This is what one teddy bear ear looks like.

**9.** Repeat this process with the other 1-inch bubble to form the other ear.

 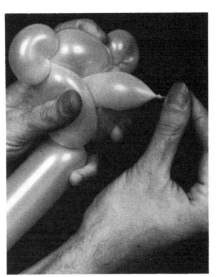 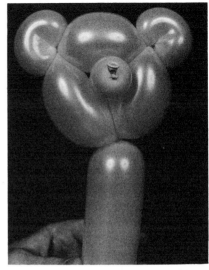

**10.** Push the nose (the end with the knot) halfway back through the three 2-inch bubbles. Remember to roll the 2-inch bubbles around the nose.

**11.** Give a gentle tug on the knot to release a little extra balloon at the knot.

**12.** This is what the teddy bear's head looks like.

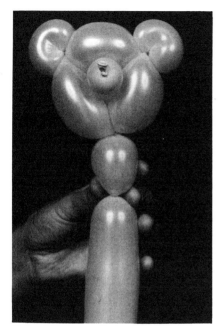

**13.** Make a 1-inch bubble for the neck.

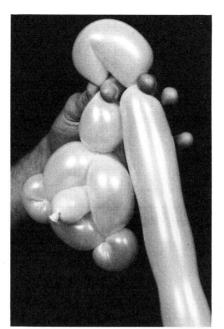

**14.** Make a 2-inch bubble and fold it in half, as you did for the elephant's ears.

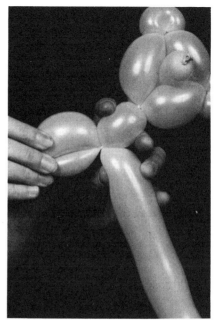

**15.** Join the folded bubble at its ends with a *locking twist.*

**16.** This is what one teddy bear arm looks like.

**17.** Repeat this process with a second 2-inch bubble for the second arm.

**18.** Make a 2-inch bubble for the body.

**19.** Make another folded 2-inch bubble for the teddy bear's leg. This is the same folded bubble that you have just made for the teddy bear's arms. Join it on its ends with a *locking twist.*

**20.** Make another folded 2-inch bubble for the second leg. Join it on its ends, and be sure to leave a little bubble for a tail.

**21.** This is what the balloon teddy bear looks like.

# TULIP

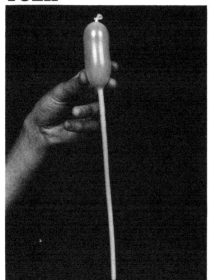

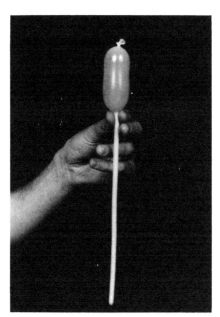

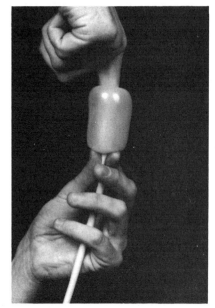

**1.** Blow up a balloon with just 1½ inches of air. Tie a knot.

**2.** Hold the balloon by the stem with your left hand, just below the bubble.

**3.** With the index finger of your right hand, push the knot down into the bubble, all the way down into the stem.

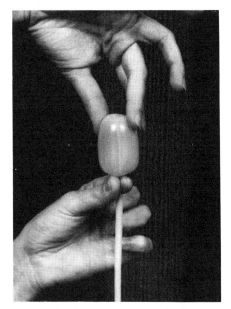

**4.** Grab the knot through the stem with your left-hand fingers and hold onto it.

**5.** Carefully slide your right index finger out of the balloon.

**6.** Hold the bubble with your right hand, and turn it around a few times. This will lock the knot in place.

**7.** This is a balloon tulip.

**8.** Slip the tail end of the tulip into one of the teddy bear's folded balloon arms.

**9.** Pull it all the way through, and you have a balloon teddy bear holding a balloon tulip.

# BUILDING YOUR REPERTOIRE

Balloon-animal twisting has unlimited possibilities. With practice and a little imagination, you should soon be able to create a whole zoo! There are many different ways to use balloon creations: as bathtub toys, household decorations, gifts, dashboard statements, party favors. Nor should your experiments be limited to animals. You can make all sorts of things to wear (such as the hat listed in the beginner section), or create a balloon facsimile of just about anything. Abstract balloon art is also attractive.

I hope your new skills bring you years of enjoyment, if not fame and fortune.

# MAIL-ORDER SOURCES

If you can't find balloons or a pump in your local magic, joke, or novelty shop, try one of these mail-order sources. All balloons are $15.00 a bag, postage and handling included, and come packaged 144 balloons to a bag. They are the highest-quality premium balloons available. All pumps are $6.00 each, postage and handling included. Please use U.S. currency on all orders and include an additional $3.00 postage on all orders going outside the United States.

**Balloon Animals***
P.O. Box 711
Medford, MA 02155

**Balloonology***
P.O. Box 301
Cambridge, MA 02238

*Massachusetts residents add 5 percent sales tax (75¢ per bag, 30¢ per pump).